ROBOTS SAVING LIVES

WILL ROBOTS
TAKE OVER
THE WORLD?

Louise Spilsbury

CHERITON
CHILDREN'S BOOKS

Published in 2024 by **Cheriton Children's Books**
1 Bank Drive West, Shrewsbury, Shropshire, SY3 9DJ, UK

© 2024 Cheriton Children's Books

First Edition

Author: Louise Spilsbury
Designer: Paul Myerscough
Editor: Jennifer Sanderson
Proofreader: Katie Dicker

Picture credits: Cover: Shutterstock/Elnur (top), Shutterstock/Ociacia (left). Inside: p1: Shutterstock/Iokanan VFX Studios, p4: Shutterstock/Suwin, p5: Shutterstock/Alexander Limbach, p6b: Shutterstock/Miriam Doerr Martin Frommherz, p6t: InTouchHealth, p7: Shutterstock/Getmilitaryphotos, p8: Shutterstock/Phonlamai Photo, p9: Shutterstock/Helloabc, p10: Shutterstock/Phonlamai Photo, p11: Shutterstock/Andrey Popov, p12: Shutterstock/Iokanan VFX Studios, p13: Shutterstock, p14: Shutterstock/Riopatuca, p15: Shutterstock/Have a nice day Photo, pp16-17: Intuitive Surgical, p18: Vicarious Surgical, p19: Shutterstock/Andrey Suslov, p20: Shutterstock/Archy13, p21b: Shutterstock/Fizkes, p21c: Given Imaging, p22: Shutterstock/Fusebulb/Marko Aliaksandr, p23: Shutterstock/SciePro, p24: Shutterstock/Halawi, p25: Shutterstock/Miriam Doerr Martin Frommherz, p26: Shutterstock/Onairp, p27: Shutterstock/PaO STUDIO, p28: Wikimedia Commons/Aldebaran Robotics/ubahnverleih, p29: Shutterstock/Stock-Asso, p30: Wikimedia Commons/Club First Robotics, p31: Shutterstock/Scharfsinn, p32: Shutterstock/AlexandrinaZ, p33: Xenex, p34l: Flickr/EK Robotics, p34r: El Camino Hospital, California, p35: Shutterstock/Miriam Doerr Martin Frommherz, p36: Shutterstock/Andy Dean Photography, p37: CFC Insights, p38: KUKA Group, p39: Matia Robotics, p40: Shutterstock/Nimito, p41: Shutterstock/Viorel Kurnosov, p42: Shutterstock/Gorodenkoff, p43: Shutterstock/Olesia Bilkei, p44: Shutterstock/VE Studio, p45: Shutterstock/Gorodenkoff.

Printed in China

Please visit our website,
www.cheritonchildrensbooks.com
to see more of our high-quality books.

CONTENTS

Chapter 1 _Robotic Doctors_.....................................4
Robot Takeover: Doctor on the Go..................10

Chapter 2 _Bot Surgeons_..12
Robot Takeover: Robotic Surgeon on Duty....18

Chapter 3 _Targeting Treatments_...................20
Robot Takeover: Drug Dispensers....................24

Chapter 4 _Robotic Nurses_................................26
Robot Takeover: Robotic Nurse in Action......30

Chapter 5 _Robotic Teams_................................32
Robot Takeover: Drones to the Rescue.........36

Chapter 6 _Rehab Robots_..................................38
Robot Takeover: Robotic Exoskeletons.........44

Glossary...46
Find Out More...47
Index and About the Author.............................48

Chapter 1

ROBOTIC DOCTORS

Imagine you are a patient arriving at the hospital where there aren't any doctors. There are no nurses to be seen. The entire medical unit is run by robots. Each stage of care through the hospital is carried out by a computer, machine, or robot. You sign yourself in on a touch pad and a robot asks you your **symptoms**, than gives you a **diagnosis**. Robots perform surgery, give injections, and even fit **prosthetic limbs**. Could this be what health care would look like in the future?

ROBOTS IN ACTION

Robots are already an important part of the health care workforce. They are changing the way that clinics and hospitals prevent, diagnose, and treat different illnesses. They are also being used to improve the care that patients receive. For example, some medical robots do routine, or regular, jobs, which gives highly skilled human health care workers more time to do complicated tasks. Other robots can carry out surgery, help patients recover from operations or illnesses, or carry medicines inside the human body to exactly where they are needed.

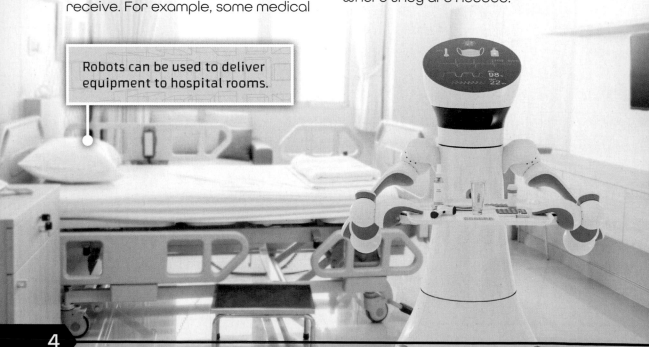

Robots can be used to deliver equipment to hospital rooms.

ROBOTS VERSUS PEOPLE

Robots can help keep people safe. For example, when treating infectious diseases that don't yet have a cure or vaccine, robots can save lives. In this situation, robots diagnosing patients reduces the risk to both the patient and the health care workers of catching the disease and passing it on. But as yet, robots don't have the ability human nurses and doctors do to understand their patients. This could include things that humans sense and question rather than hear, such as is a patient happy with their diagnosis or are there things they are *not* saying that should be considered?

BIG BOT DEBATE

Are Robotic Doctors the Future?

Some people believe robotic doctors are the future of medicine. They say robots are less likely to make mistakes and will have computer programs that contain millions of details about conditions that doctors could not possibly remember. Other people say that a robotic doctor would never be able to talk to a patient like a human or understand how they feel. Do you think robotic doctors are the future or do you believe only human doctors can help people?

In the future, there may even be **humanoid** robotic doctors that look, talk, and act like human doctors.

TELEMEDICS AT WORK

There's a new type of doctor patrolling the wards! Telemedics are robots that travel by themselves to different patients' rooms in the hospital. They help doctors speak to, examine, and diagnose patients from far away. Telemedics are a huge help to patients who need a diagnosis from specialists who are not in the same place. In the past, a patient would have to wait to be transferred to a different hospital to see the specialist. Today, patients can consult with a specialist immediately, with no wait.

ROVING ASSISTANT

Telemedics move on wheels and can find their own way to patients. They are covered in **sensors** that stop them from bumping into people or things. When a patient needs a diagnosis, a telemedic displays a live video of the doctor's face from its screen. Telemedics have advanced cameras, lenses, and microphones that enable specialists to see, hear, and speak with patients as if they were at their bedside. The robots can give doctors access to computer records of medical images or the results of tests that patients may have undergone.

Telemedics allow specialist doctors to diagnose patients from a distance so patients do not have to change hospitals.

In the future, robots will be able to carry out many tasks.

ROBOTS RISING UP!

In the future, telemedic robots could be saving lives on battlefields. Soldiers injured in **remote** places need help fast. Military doctors could use telemedics to supply instant medical records of their patients and get advice from specialists on how to treat wounded soldiers.

Telemedics can travel with armies, ready to be switched on and head into action when they are needed.

TELEMEDICS SAVE LIVES

Telemedics are not only incredibly useful but they also save lives. For example, a patient may be in a remote hospital where there is a shortage of doctors, and is too sick to travel to a city hospital for help. By consulting with a specialist via a telemedic robot that can see and question the patient in detail, the patient might get the life-saving diagnosis they need.

IT'S AN EMERGENCY!

In an incident in which many people are injured, for example, a multiple car crash or a terrorist attack, hospital emergency rooms fill up with wounded people very quickly. Before patients can be treated, they need to be triaged. This is when patients are checked over to see how urgently they need treatment. Telemedics can help doctors from different cities or even different countries examine patients in such an emergency. A quick diagnosis and a decision about which patients need the most urgent care can make the difference between life and death.

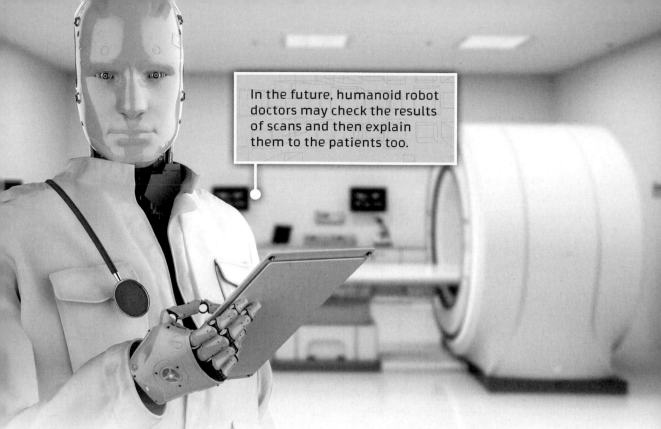

In the future, humanoid robot doctors may check the results of scans and then explain them to the patients too.

ROBOTS ON REPORT

It's not always easy to tell what is wrong with someone just by looking at them or having them describe their symptoms. Medical imaging is a process by which high-tech machines take pictures or films of a patient's insides to help doctors figure out what the problem is. These images can show infections, swelling, injury, or disease without the doctor having to cut open and look inside a patient's body. Robots are helping interpret scans and images to detect, diagnose, and treat a variety of diseases.

IMAGES FROM THE INSIDE

Medical imaging is amazing. X-rays are used to photograph bones and teeth. Computed tomography (CAT or CT) scans take hundreds of X-ray pictures of the patient's bones, organs, and tissues. Magnetic resonance imaging (MRI) provides even more detailed pictures of a patient's insides. The problem is that checking these images carefully is a time-consuming task that is usually done by experienced specialists and doctors. Sometimes, humans make mistakes, perhaps because they are tired. Sometimes there is a slight difference in the way a medical problem looks, so a doctor may miss it. This is where artificial intelligence (AI) can help.

AI IN ACTION

AI is a branch of computer science in which computers perform tasks that normally need human intelligence. The computers are programmed to complete the task using algorithms. Algorithms are step-by-step mathematical instructions and rules. For example, by using algorithms, the machine can detect specific **abnormalities** or patterns, such as **tumors** and areas of swelling. Some people think that AI systems are just as effective as humans in reading and diagnosing scans and images, and sometimes, even more so.

FAST AND ACCURATE

Robots can analyze X-rays and scans, freeing up health care workers to do other things that robots cannot, such as reassuring sick patients or carrying out tricky surgeries. A fast and accurate diagnosis also means people will have shorter waiting times to get results. This will reduce infection rates and increase patients' chances of survival.

To keep medical staff safe, robots can be used to deliver sanitizer and medicines to infectious patients.

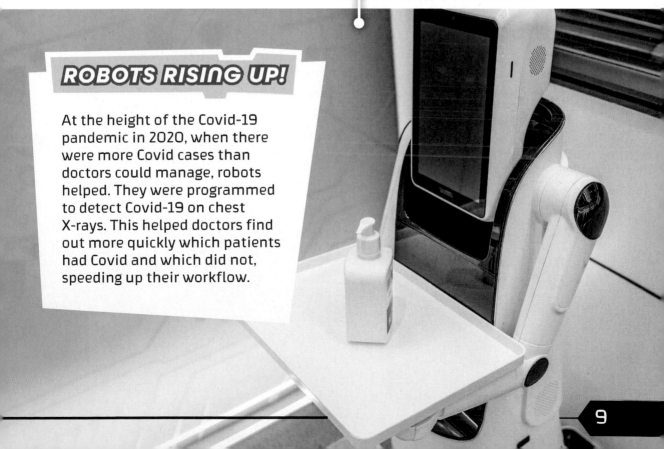

ROBOTS RISING UP!

At the height of the Covid-19 pandemic in 2020, when there were more Covid cases than doctors could manage, robots helped. They were programmed to detect Covid-19 on chest X-rays. This helped doctors find out more quickly which patients had Covid and which did not, speeding up their workflow.

ROBOT TAKEOVER:
DOCTOR ON THE GO

It's always important to get an early diagnosis for a health condition. The sooner someone knows what is wrong with them, the sooner they can make healthier choices or take medicines to prevent the condition becoming worse. Yet some people delay getting advice. They put off going to the doctor about a health concern because they're worried about wasting the doctor's time or they feel embarrassed to talk about the problem. In the future, PETRA the robot may be able to help.

Talk to PETRA!

PETRA stands for Prescreening Experience Through Robot Assessment. PETRA is a robot that can diagnose different health conditions, such as telling if someone is at risk of developing **diabetes**. PETRA asks the patient a set of questions to which the patient should answer "yes" or "no." Depending on the answers, the robot will figure out the likelihood of them having or developing a medical condition. Scientists hope that PETRA will be able to diagnose more and more conditions.

Listen to PETRA

The idea behind a robot like PETRA is that after it has told you what is wrong with you, it then suggests what you can do next. It might advise you on things you can do to improve your health, such as doing more exercise. It could even help patients book a doctor's appointment.

In the future, you won't have to book a doctor's appointment to get a diagnosis. You could interact with a robot at your local drug store, shopping mall, or airport to find out if you have an illness.

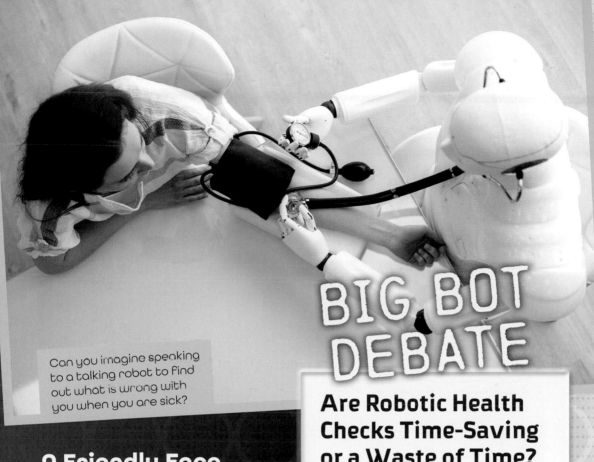

Can you imagine speaking to a talking robot to find out what is wrong with you when you are sick?

BIG BOT DEBATE

A Friendly Face

Social robots are robots with faces that speak with human-sounding voices. Scientists believe that people are more willing to share information with social robots and act as if they are talking to humans. PETRA looks, feels, and acts more human than many other robots. It speaks in a friendly way to encourage people to tell it personal information and their health worries.

Are Robotic Health Checks Time-Saving or a Waste of Time?

Some people argue that robotic health checks are a good thing because they save medical professionals' time in the long run. They say more people will get diagnosed, and having a robot to make diagnoses frees up health care staff to do other things. Other people disagree. They say that humans are complicated and there is not always a single answer to a medical problem. A human doctor can sense when something else is wrong, perhaps from a patient's face or mood, which a robot is unable to do. Do you think robotic health checks are the way forward or do you believe only human doctors should perform these tasks?

Chapter 2

BOT SURGEONS

When most people think of having an operation, they imagine surgeons in gowns and masks, working on a patient with their own gloved hands. But things are changing. Robotic surgeons are already in action around the world. At present, human surgeons remain in control, with the machine mimicking, or copying, their hand movements. But as robots improve, could it be possible for the robots to be fully in charge?

CONTROLLING SURGICAL ROBOTS

Most surgical robots consist of a camera arm and mechanical arms with surgical tools attached to them. The human surgeon controls the arms from a computer console nearby. The cameras give the human surgeon a **high-definition**, **magnified** view of the surgery. From the console, the human surgeon is also able to make both the mechanical arm and the surgical instruments move to carry out the operation.

In the future, robotic surgeons may be able to carry out some incredibly delicate operations.

ROBOTS RISING UP!

Robotic surgeons allow doctors to carry out many types of complicated and delicate operations with increased **precision** and control. Using robotic surgeons helps human surgeons better see the parts of the body they are working on. That means less pain and faster healing for patients.

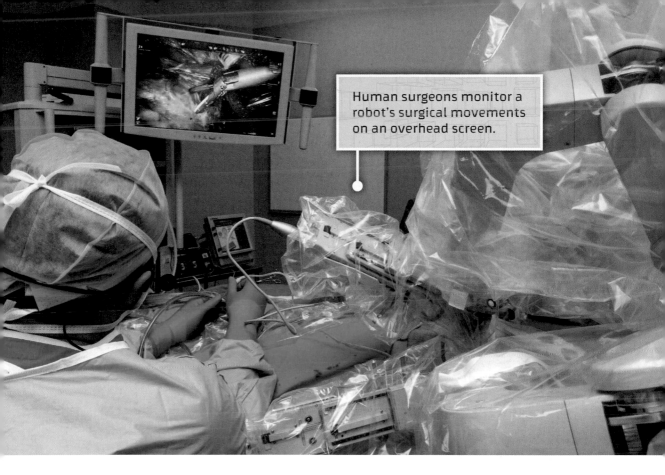

Human surgeons monitor a robot's surgical movements on an overhead screen.

MAKING THE CUT

There are two types of surgery: open and minimally invasive. Open surgery is when a surgeon works directly on a patient. It involves making a large incision, or cut, in the patient's skin and muscles, so that the surgeon can see the parts of the body they are working on. Minimally invasive surgery is done without making a large incision in the patient's body. The entire operation is carried out through tiny holes instead. Robots are used mainly in minimally invasive surgery.

ROBOTIC SURGEONS SAVE LIVES

Robotic surgery makes minimally invasive surgery possible. This type of surgery causes less damage to the body than open surgery. There is less blood loss for the patient and there is less pain because there's a smaller wound to heal. Smaller incisions also mean patients have far fewer complications. There is less risk patients will get infections around the wound. The patients make a quicker recovery so their time in hospital is reduced. This frees up hospital beds and the doctors' time for other patients.

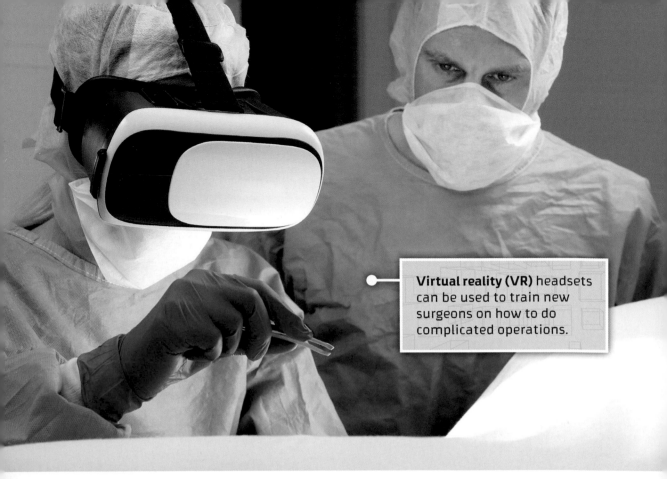

Virtual reality (VR) headsets can be used to train new surgeons on how to do complicated operations.

SURGERY BY BOT

VR is computer technology that makes a person feel like they are somewhere else. This incredibly smart tech is being used in some hospitals. Using VR, human surgeons can control a robot to make it do exactly what they want it to, precisely, quickly, and safely. A robotic surgeon is linked to the human surgeon using a VR headset and hand controllers, so every action the robot makes, no matter how small, is started and controlled by the human surgeon throughout.

IN TRAINING

When surgeons are training, they can learn, practice, and run through different procedures using VR, before they go into an actual operating theater. Lifelike images and video, and haptic feedback technology make their experience feel like the real thing. Haptic feedback technology gives the trainees physical sensations that they would experience during an operation—for example, feeling the vibration of a saw on bone when the bone is being cut.

SURGEONS WITH X-RAY VISION?

Some surgeons are using augmented reality (AR) technology to help them operate. AR uses special glasses to give a surgeon X-ray vision by combining computer-generated images with their actual view of the real world. It's like an enhanced version of the real world by adding computer-generated elements, sounds, and other sensations. This helps a surgeon know exactly where to make incisions or insert implants. For example, in surgery on a patient's spine, AR allows surgeons to see the spine in three-dimensions (3D) through the skin.

FAST LEARNERS

AR is also used by trainee surgeons practicing operations. As well as being a safe way to train, all of the movements a trainee makes are tracked in real time. This means they can see what they did wrong or how they can improve. It's like giving humans robotic skills.

ROBOTS RISING UP!

By learning to do surgeries using VR and AR, surgeons also learn the skills they will need to control robotic surgeons that will assist them in operations in the future.

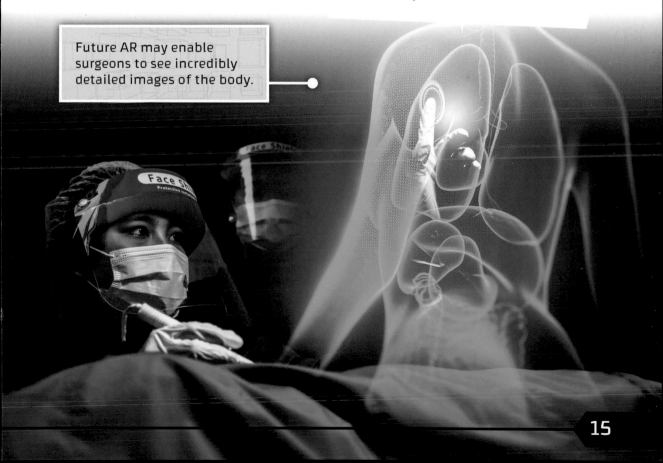

Future AR may enable surgeons to see incredibly detailed images of the body.

SURGICAL ROBOTS IN ACTION

Surgical robots, such as the da Vinci robot, are usually made up of two separate parts. The first part is the tower. The tower has up to four robotic arms that sit on a wheeled base. The tower is placed over the patient during surgery. The second part of the robot is the console, which is where the human surgeon sits and controls the operation.

HOW IT WORKS

A patient lies on the operating table and the tower is placed over them. Three of the arms do the surgery through tiny incisions in the patient. The arms can move in different directions. They can move rather like a human arm but with the improvement of a **multi-jointed** wrist. Each arm can hold a variety of tools.

EYES INSIDE

A fourth arm holds an endoscope. Endoscopes are thin, tubelike instruments used to look inside the body. They produce a clear, 3D image of where the operation is happening. A video feed of what the surgeon sees is shown on a screen so the other medics in the operating theater can see what is going on.

The da Vinci performs millions of surgeries around the world each year. It repairs heart valves so that hearts continue to beat. It removes diseased sections of an intestine so that it can continue to function.

ROBOTS RISING UP!

The da Vinci makes it possible for a human surgeon to pick up a surgical instrument and cut into a patient hundreds of miles away. From a console in the hospital in one place, a surgeon can control a robotic surgeon that does the work of slicing, stitching, and other surgical jobs on the other side of the country.

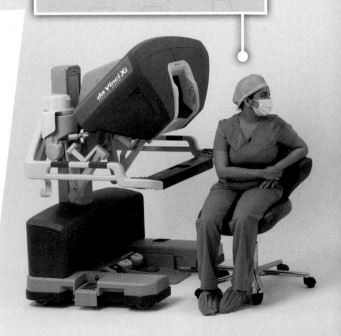

SURGEON IN CONTROL

The human surgeon sitting at the console watches a screen showing a magnified view of what the endoscope sees. They put their forefinger (the finger next to the thumb) and thumb into circular sensors. Every movement the surgeon makes sends signals to a computer. For example, they use a pinching movement to make surgical tools go up and down.

The computer tells the robotic arms where and how to move. Robotic arms mimic even slight movements that the human surgeon makes.

CUTTING-EDGE TECHNOLOGY

The narrow tips of da Vinci's arms can be fitted with different tools. These include scissors and scalpels, which are very sharp knives, for cutting and slicing, and a tool that heats up to seal bleeding blood vessels. It can also use tools that grip and move tissue out of the way, and grippers that hold needles for stitching incisions.

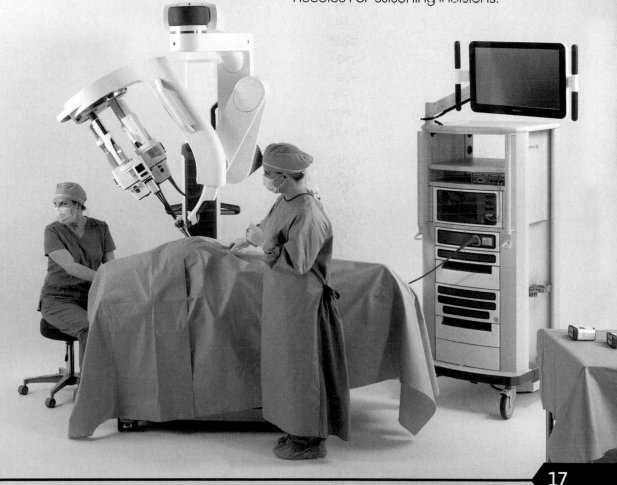

ROBOT TAKEOVER:
ROBOTIC SURGEON ON DUTY

In a movie titled *Fantastic Voyage*, doctors shrink in size to travel within a man's body in order to save him. As a child, this movie inspired the designer of a new robotic surgeon, and now the designer wants human surgeons to feel like they too are traveling in a body.

A New Mini-Bot

Although the Vicarious Surgical robot is not in use yet, it is being trained to do its first operation via the abdomen. This miniature, tube-shaped robot is so small it can pass through a single, tiny hole in the body. A camera and two robotic instruments can be passed through this hole to help the human surgeon controlling it to see as much as possible, and to be precise. Surgeons remotely control the tools using VR headsets.

Taking It All In

Each of the Vicarious robot's two arms have 28 sensors. The arms can move in any direction and are designed to mimic a human surgeon's natural upper-body movements, from shoulders to elbows and wrists. The camera shows the inside of the patient in 3D on the VR and can look in all directions. It can roll and it can move in and out, even backward, to look at the incision made in the body.

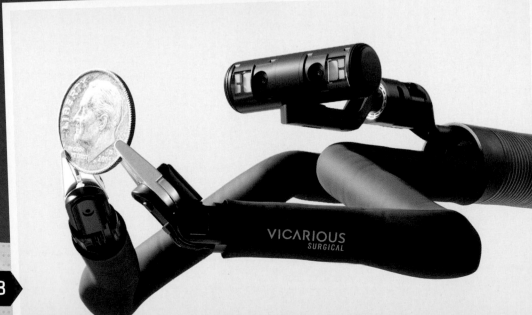

Bot surgeons have tools such as grippers on their arms that can perform precise movements.

VICARIOUS
SURGICAL

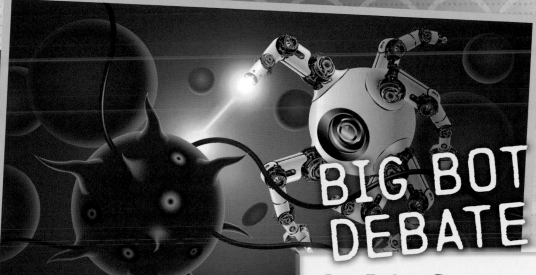

One day in the future, tiny robots may be able to carry out surgical operations on precise locations inside the body.

BIG BOT DEBATE

Working from the Inside

Unlike some robotic surgeons, the idea of the Vicarious Surgical robot is that it enters through that single incision that is smaller than a dime. Then, all of the robot's movements happen inside the patient. This means the robot can move more freely as it works because it doesn't have the skin, muscles, and fat of the abdomen to deal with. This also reduces the risk of anything knocking a performing robotic surgeon in the theater.

Are Robot Surgeons Safer than Humans?

Some people believe that even complicated surgeries will one day be performed by autonomous robotic surgeons. Autonomous robots move and work completely by themselves with no human control. They say that humans are far from perfect and there's always a risk they'll make a mistake during surgery. Therefore robotic doctors are safer and will save more lives. Other people disagree. They argue that robots can help health care workers but that it would not be safe to allow them to do operations alone. The human body is complex and robots that are programmed to do one type of operation would not recognize changes in the body that an experienced human surgeon would. Do you think robotic surgeons are safer than humans or would you trust only a human surgeon?

Chapter 3

TARGETING TREATMENTS

Doctors have a range of technology, such as scanners, to help locate, or find, areas inside the body that need treatment. But targeting these places can be tricky. Powerful drugs such as those used to treat cancerous tumors can damage healthy tissue. And the **side effects** of the treatment can also add to the patient's suffering. Remarkable robots are in use that can travel inside the body. They can take images to pinpoint problem areas—and deliver the drugs to where they are needed.

A ROBOTIC PILL

PillCam is a tiny robot that can be swallowed. It is capsule-shaped, like a tablet that people swallow for a headache. It is around 1 inch (2.5 cm) long and weighs less than 0.14 ounces (4 g). Once swallowed, PillCam moves through the stomach and intestines, just as food naturally does. It takes around eight hours to

New robotic capsules like this one will be capable of carrying out examinations and treating diseases inside the body.

pass through the body. PillCam has a battery-powered video camera with a light. The camera takes images in high-resolution with a wide-angle view so it can clearly see the insides of the gut.

SMART FILMING

PillCam normally takes four frames, or images, per second. Software in the recorder automatically compares the images with a **database** of pictures of common signs of gut illnesses. This can help speed up a diagnosis. If the system picks up on a problem, the camera increases its speed to 35 frames per second. This helps record a clear, accurate image of the problem location. Doctors download the video and use it to devise a treatment plan.

ROBOTS RISING UP!

MASCE is a flexible robot that operators can guide through a body using magnets that are outside the person. The robot can open and close a hatch to deliver a precise amount of a drug to a tumor or other target site. It can also open tiny grippers that are like claws. These claws can open and close to take a small tissue **sample** for testing. A **silicon** brush then sweeps the claws with the sample they contain.

PillCam is small so can be taken with a glass of water like a regular pill, but it definitely needs to be swallowed whole!

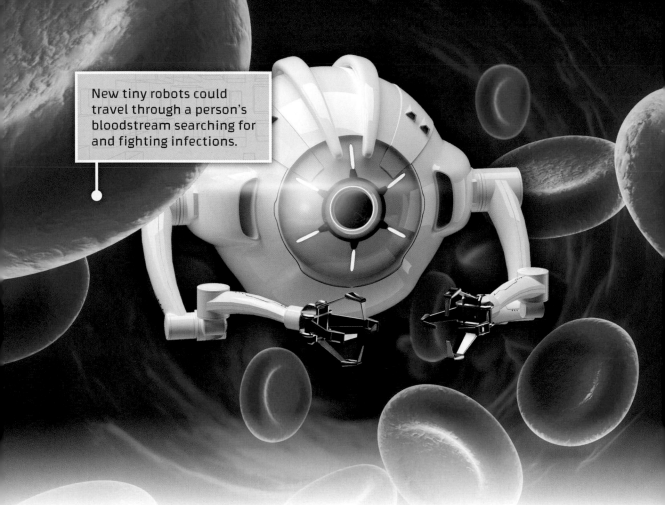

New tiny robots could travel through a person's bloodstream searching for and fighting infections.

INNER VOYAGERS

Robots that take treatment to exactly where it's needed in the body are not limited to targeting the gut. A new generation of bots will soon be traveling in some of the other remarkable systems inside the body. The robots are designed to explore the veins and arteries of the **circulatory system**. Target bots will even move along the spinal cord and other parts of the **nervous system**. These routes give access to nearly all parts of the human body.

ON A ROLL

The microroller is a mini robot that mimics a white blood cell. White blood cells are responsible for fighting infection. The microroller is spherical and has a glass core, or middle. One half of it is coated with a magnetic layer to allow a magnetic controller to move and steer it. The other half is coated with an anti-cancer drug and antibodies. Antibodies stick to particular unwanted substances or objects in the body, such as cancer cells in a tumor. The antibodies help the microroller target the tumor to deliver an anti-cancer drug.

GETTING ON YOUR NERVES!

Moving through the nervous system is tricky: Nerves ripple and twist, and have steep slopes. MANiAC is a specialist robot for moving around the nervous system. It is a very small, soft-bodied spherical bot. Tiny flexible rods inside can push, pull, or twist the outer shell. The rods are magnetic and they are controlled from a controller on the outside. MANiAC can be made to tumble through the nervous system to deliver medication to where it's needed.

ROBOTS RISING UP!

Scientists have developed mini-bots that can swim inside the lungs to treat **pneumonia**. They engineered **algae** cells speckled with **antibiotic**-filled dots. The algae swim down the fluid in the windpipe into the lungs. A special coating on the dots protects the antibiotic and also reduces the white blood cells causing swelling in the lungs. Taking the antibiotics to the infection sites by mini-bot is a more effective treatment than an injection. It also requires less antibiotic to do the job.

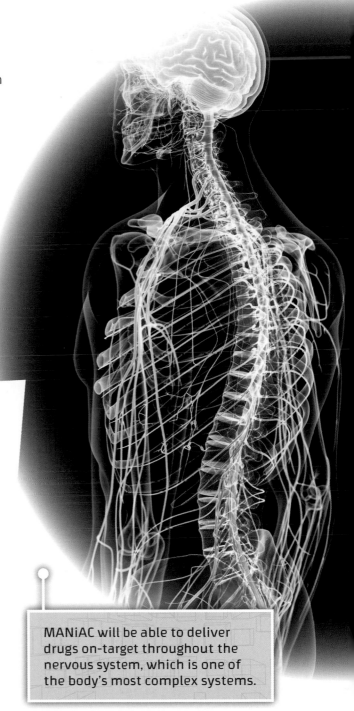

MANiAC will be able to deliver drugs on-target throughout the nervous system, which is one of the body's most complex systems.

Delivering drugs to specific places in the body is vital, but making sure those drugs are the correct ones is even more important. Unfortunately, mistakes are sometimes made. Some of these mistakes are caused by patients accidentally being given the wrong dose or the incorrect drug. In big, busy hospitals, pharmacies deal with a lot of drugs at any one time. A team of human pharmacists may struggle to keep up with the demand. When rushed, these pharmacists are more likely to make mistakes. Drug-dispensing robots can help!

Robots Run the Pharmacy

Modern pharmacies, especially in busy hospitals, have robots that handle thousands of drugs. In some, a robotic arm can locate specific drugs by using barcodes, like those you see on the side of products in a store. Each patient's **prescription** has a unique barcode.

A picking arm with a barcode scanner ensures the robot finds and picks the correct medicine from the shelves. Then, medical staff or robots take the medicines to where they are needed in the hospital.

Robots can automatically pick prescriptions for many specific patients, day and night, and with an incredibly high level of accuracy.

Robots Pack the Shelves

Making sure a pharmacy is always well-stocked is vital. Robotic systems can also ensure that there is the right amount of medicines on pharmacy shelves at all times. They can keep a record of changes each time a drug or medicine is dispensed. The robot can then alert staff when it is time to restock drugs. Medicines also have date-of-manufacture information built into their barcodes, so pharmacy robots can make sure that medicines are used within safe time limits.

In the future, all hospitals and care homes may have robots that select and pack medicines and robots that then deliver the medicines to the patient, too.

BIG BOT DEBATE

Are Robotic Pharmacists Useful or Useless?

Some people say that robotic pharmacists are useful because there is less chance of robots making a mistake when selecting the amount and type of medicine. Robots also cut the amount of time that human pharmacists spend finding, picking, and packing prescriptions, giving them more time to spend dealing with specific patient drug needs and finding out about new drug therapies. Other people argue that even the smallest mistakes when dealing with complex medication can be fatal and the risks of using a drug-dispensing robot are too high. Do you believe robotic pharmacists are useful or do you think they pose a risk and only humans can be trusted?

Chapter 4

ROBOTIC NURSES

Hospitals are busy places, and nurses have to deal with many patients every day. They have a very important job to do but their medical work is often interrupted by carrying out tasks such as collecting things that their patients need. That is where robots can step in.

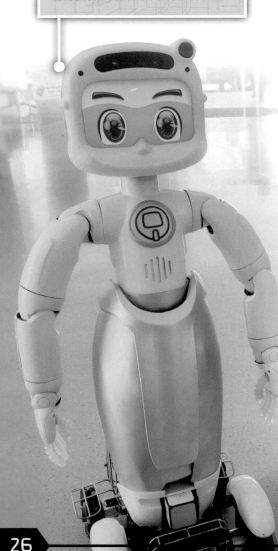

Robotic nurses are designed to help patients and assist medical staff in their work.

STAND AND DELIVER

Today, delivery robots are saving nurses from spending hours collecting or delivering things around the hospital. These robots can collect and deliver samples, medicines, and devices on their ward rounds. Some delivery robots have a locked cabinet so that only nurses with the code can open it to access the drugs inside.

SUPER SENSORS

Hospital delivery robots can travel around by themselves. They find their way using a combination of sensors to see into the distance and to avoid obstacles, such as people, wheelchairs, and beds. Some have LiDAR systems, which scan and send out short **laser** beams of light that bounce back when they hit an obstacle. Sonar technology sends **pulses** of sound that bounce back off the closest objects. These technologies tell the robot where things are in the surrounding area.

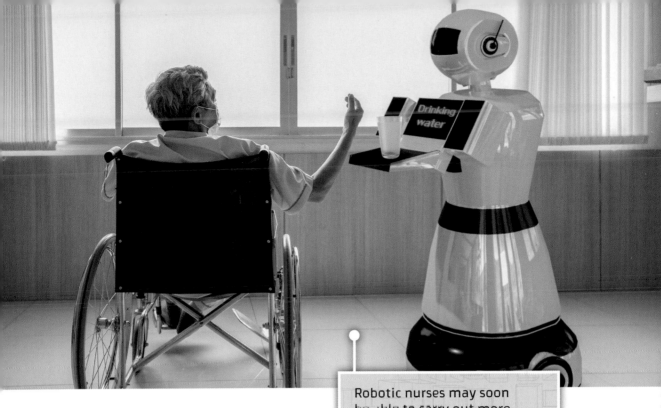

Robotic nurses may soon be able to carry out more simple tasks, such as ensuring patients drink enough water.

MOVE OVER FOR MOXI!

Moxi is a 4-feet- (1.2 m) tall robot that travels between different floors of the hospital. Its main job is to deliver medication 24 hours a day but it can even travel to the gift store to pick up items for patients. Moxi can tackle doors and elevators with its robotic arm. It stores goods in its base, which contains three locked drawers.

THE LITTLE BOT THAT CAN

Using cell phones, nurses can call or securely send text messages to Moxi robots. Once a Moxi robot receives the request, it responds within five minutes with a status update and an estimated time of arrival. Then it zips through the hospital's hallways and corridors to its destination. One hospital reported that in the first six weeks of use, Moxi had saved its nurses nearly 300 miles (483 km) of walking!

ROBOTS RISING UP!

Moxi is equipped with AI, which means it learns where to go in a new hospital. The more Moxi is used, the more it learns and adapts to its surroundings and specific systems in the hospital.

MEET MEDi!

At some children's hospitals, patients are not greeted by a human nurse. Instead they are met by a cute robot with a big smile called MEDi. MEDi is only 2 feet (60 cm) tall but this small robot has a big job to do: MEDi helps children feel more relaxed and calm when they have to go to the hospital for an operation or treatment.

MEDi MOODS

There are MEDi robots in some wards where children are having uncomfortable procedures, tests, or injections. Being hurt or having a serious illness can be worrying or scary so MEDi makes things more fun. It greets children and introduces itself. It explains what tests the children are going to have so they know what is going on. Then MEDi takes their mind off things by telling stories, dancing, and playing games. MEDi can even offer its patients high-fives!

ROBOTS RISING UP!

When people are stressed, they feel discomfort and pain more strongly because they are already tense. By lowering children's stress levels and making them feel more relaxed, MEDi has been able to reduce their pain.

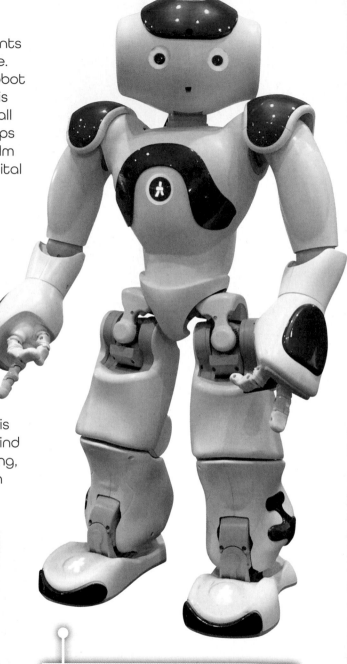

Laughing at MEDi performing a silly dance can distract patients from getting injections and undergoing other unsettling procedures.

SEND FOR STEVIE!

People are living longer than ever, and that means there will be more elderly people who need care in nursing homes and retirement communities. When people are older and less able to move around, they can get bored and lonely. Stevie is a robot designed to help. Stevie can roam about and talk to people autonomously, for example, in the lobby of a nursing home or while care home residents are playing a game. Stevie has face and voice recognition, which means it can talk to people directly, and understand and reply to commands.

STEVIE THE TIME-SAVER

The great thing about a robot like Stevie is that if a patient is happy talking to it, that frees up human nurses and carers to do other jobs. Alternatively, Stevie can also do jobs that free up human nurses to spend more time talking to their elderly patients. For example, Stevie can take over the job of running a games evening, meaning that carers are free to chat with and help the residents instead.

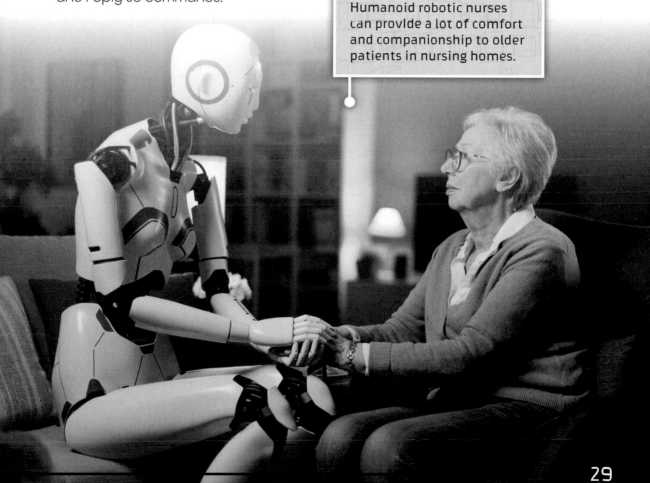

Humanoid robotic nurses can provide a lot of comfort and companionship to older patients in nursing homes.

ROBOT TAKEOVER:
ROBOTIC NURSE IN ACTION

"Lovely, intelligent, and well-dressed—" that's how one patient described her friendly nurse, named Grace. But Grace is not a human nurse. Grace is a humanoid robot that helps out at long-term care homes. Grace can assist doctors and nurses, and can also chat to elderly people living in the care home to combat loneliness and brighten their day.

A Robotic Companion

Loneliness causes many health problems, from **depression** to illnesses such as heart disease and cancer. In fact, loneliness is one of the biggest causes of death and disability across the world. Grace roams about the care home, talking to people and asking them questions. Grace is programmed to speak three languages —English, Mandarin, and Cantonese—and can socialize and spend time chatting with patients in the nursing home.

A Robot with Feelings?

Grace can recognize and respond to seven human emotions and can mirror the facial expressions of whomever she is talking to. So, if someone is looking sad, she will look sad too. This makes people believe that the robot understands their feelings, more like a human nurse would.

Robotic nurses are proving popular with patients, and the more lifelike they are, the better!

Robotic nurses may not feel human but they can help keep patients calm before surgeries and other procedures.

BIG BOT DEBATE

A Friendly Smile

Humans feel more comfortable talking to robots that look more like people, so Grace has a humanlike face and hair, and even wears a blue nurse's uniform. Grace can move not only its eyes but also its neck and hands. It can even **simulate** the action of more than 48 major facial muscles, to make it more **expressive**.

Assisting Doctors

Nurse Grace can also help doctors diagnose illnesses and deliver treatments. Grace is equipped with sensors, including a camera in its chest that can be used to detect a patient's temperature and **pulse**. Grace uses AI to diagnose problems using the readings it takes from a patient.

Are Robotic Nurses a Good Replacement for Human Nurses?

Some people say that talking to a robot might not be quite as good as talking to a real person but when staff are busy, a robotic nurse can give people the attention they need. Other people say that nothing can replace human conversation and care, and that instead of spending money on robotic nurses, hospitals should be paying to train human nurses and to increase their wages. Do you think robotic nurses have a part to play or do you think we should invest in human nurses?

Chapter 5

ROBOTIC TEAMS

Hospitals are large, complicated facilities with many staff moving quickly through the corridors to keep everyone healthy. There are a lot of different jobs to do to make sure everything in the hospital runs smoothly, from making sure the buildings are clean and free of germs that can cause disease to delivering clean bedding and medicine to the correct wards.

ROBOT CLEANERS

Keeping hospitals clean is a vitally important job. Hospitals are suited to robotic cleaners and other robotic staff because they usually have flat, well-lit halls and floors, and elevators that robots can roll into to travel between floors. Corridors and walkways are kept clear for stretchers and carts, so there are few obstacles to get in a robot's way as it travels around.

PRECISION WORK

Robotic floor scrubbers are autonomous machines that are used to clean and maintain floors in hospitals. They usually use a combination of water, detergent, and brushes or pads to scrub and clean the floor's surface. Robotic floor scrubbers carry advanced sensors and **navigation** systems that allow them to clean every inch of a hospital floor without missing a spot and without getting lost.

Robots can do a variety of cleaning jobs throughout hospitals.

ROBOTS RISING UP!

Superbugs are germs that can cause nasty and sometimes deadly infections. Many patients catch superbugs while they are in the hospital getting treatment for another condition. Robotic cleaners can kill almost all germs, even those horrible superbugs.

ALWAYS ON DUTY

Robotic cleaners can be programmed to clean specific areas at set times. They can also be controlled remotely. They can be loaded with floor plan information, allowing them to clean the main corridors at night time. Most also have expressive eyes and the ability to speak, so they can interact with patients, visitors, and any hospital staff they meet while cleaning.

MAKING LIGHT WORK OF CLEANING

Robot cleaners also clean by blasting **ultraviolet (UV)** light that is 25,000 times more powerful than sunlight, over surfaces. Germs are tiny living things and UV light harms them and stops them from being able to multiply and spread. Robots can focus UV light on difficult-to-reach places, such as the folds between curtains, computer keyboards, or medical equipment, to ensure every surface is clean and germ-free.

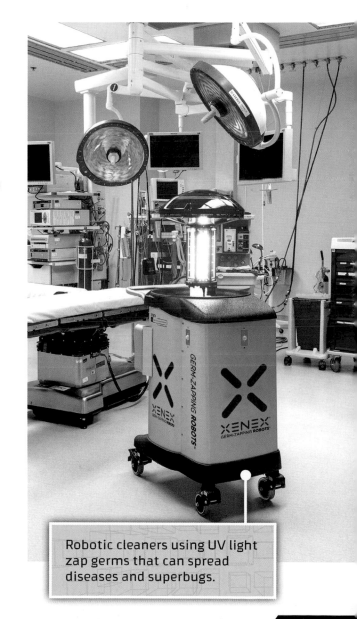

Robotic cleaners using UV light zap germs that can spread diseases and superbugs.

PORTER POWER

Porters are crucial to hospitals. They make sure important goods and items such as food and linen are delivered where they are needed. They also make sure patients are at the right place at the right time to get the treatment they need. In hospitals around the world, fleets of robotic porters are starting to carry out these tasks.

CALL PORTER-BOT

Porter-bots are able to collect a wide range of items including kitchen materials, linen, and medical supplies that they unload from specially designed bays. Battery-powered porter-bots queue at different points around the hospital, waiting for staff to call them into action. Then they speed through the tunnels and corridors, slowing down or stopping if they detect a risk of collision.

Most porter-bots can also call elevators, allowing them to deliver goods to different floors.

TUG TIME

TUG is a porter-bot that moves autonomously around the hospital, picking up and delivering patients' meals, linen, and medication. TUG follows a programmed checklist. The checklist is set up by hospital staff and it tells the robot which tasks need to be done first. TUG was named after the way it tugs, or pulls, different carts, such as heated food carts, which can be attached to its body.

Robotic porters perform delivery tasks in hospitals to give staff more time to focus on patient care.

ON THE MOVE

TUG is loaded with a map of the hospital and it also builds a highly detailed 3D map of the corridors and walkways by bouncing lasers off its surroundings. It also has sonar and infrared sensors to help it find its way around obstacles and people. TUG stands back from elevators and calls them through the hospital's wireless network, using **radio waves** to open doors.

TUG TALKS

TUG cannot hold a conversation but it can say up to 70 different phrases while performing its tasks. It can say "your deliveries are here," and it asks people to "please stand aside" when it gets onto an elevator. It also says "thank you" after it makes a delivery.

ROBOTS RISING UP!

In the not-too-distant future, porters will not need to push patients' beds to an operating theater and back. Instead, self-driving robotic beds will transport patients from the emergency room to the operating theater, and via the X-ray department if needed.

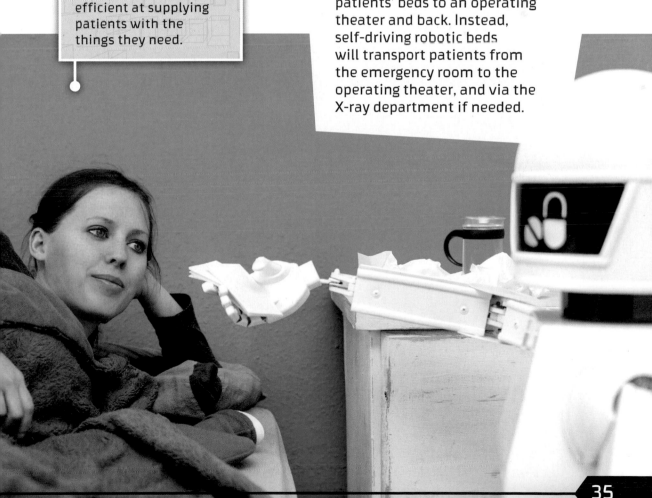

Robotic porters are very efficient at supplying patients with the things they need.

Robots are not only used to deliver supplies from one ward to another in the hospital. Some hospital staff have the job of delivering vital medicines and samples between different hospitals. This can take hours by truck or motorcycle, and the trip can be delayed by traffic hold-ups. Drones are flying robots that can make these deliveries much more quickly and save lives when doing so.

Saving Lives

Some medication, such as cancer drugs, are difficult to transport as some doses have a short shelf life. That means if it takes too long to deliver them to the hospital where a patient is waiting for them, the medicine is no longer effective. If a drone can carry the medicines in the air where there is no traffic and flying at speeds of 70 miles per hour (112 kph), the treatment will get to the patients in record time. Drones also carry samples from a patient in one hospital to a lab in another hospital, so the sample can be checked quickly. This helps doctors decide how to treat a patient and, potentially, may help to save their life.

Drones can pick up and drop off lifesaving treatment to patients on the same day.

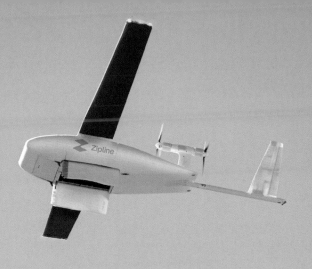

Drones can drop medicines and other medical supplies directly at patients' homes. This is especially useful to patients who may be too weak or sick to leave their homes.

Coming in to Land

Most medical drones look like small, electric airplanes. During a delivery, a drone often does not land. Instead it comes down to a low height and drops the package to the ground. The package often has a little parachute to help it land gently without damaging its contents. The drone may also carry the package at the end of a long wire so it can be lowered down to its destination. Drones have sensors that take in information about conditions such as wind speed and direction, so they can accurately drop packages within a target area about the size of a couple of parking spaces.

BIG BOT DEBATE

Are Medical Drones Good or Bad?

Some people believe medical drones are a good thing. They argue that flying bots deliver medicines more quickly and they also save fuel, which is better for the environment. Other people say drones cost a lot to buy and there is a risk that the cameras on a drone might be used to spy on people. Do you think that medical drones are useful or do you believe they could pose a risk?

Chapter 6

REHAB ROBOTS

Rehabilitation is the care and treatment that helps people get back to their lives after an injury or an operation. People may need help learning to walk again after an accident, for example. Some people who have lost or are unable to move limbs need other types of help. Rehab robots can make life-changing impacts on the lives of people who have difficulty moving around on their own.

A PHYSIO ROBOT

Getting leg muscles and joints strong and working again properly after an operation or accident, often means doing the same or similar exercises or treatments with a patient over and again. ROBERT is a robotic physiotherapist with a multi-jointed arm that can help.

ROBERT ON REPEAT

To train ROBERT, a physiotherapist performs movements on the patient, which ROBERT learns and then memorizes. After that, ROBERT can perform exactly the same movements over and over again, without getting tired, bored, or stopping to take a break.

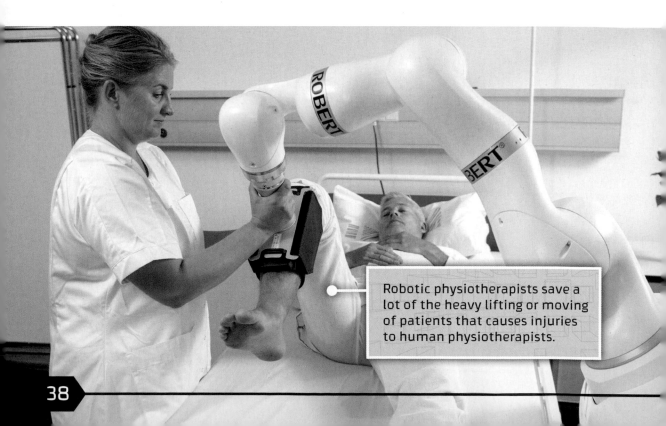

Robotic physiotherapists save a lot of the heavy lifting or moving of patients that causes injuries to human physiotherapists.

HIGH-TECH TEK!

If someone has difficulty walking or getting around, they may use a wheelchair. Wheelchairs are very useful but have some **limitations**. For example, they are not ideal for going long distances or up slopes, and they struggle with narrow doorways. It's also healthy for people in wheelchairs who can stand to get up for some time each day. A Tek robot supports people with walking disabilities in an upright position so they can independently sit, stand, and move around places that were once too difficult to get to.

GOING FOR A WALK

Patients call the Tek robot to them using a remote. They change its speed and movement with a **joystick**. As the user's body is supported, that leaves their hands free to reach high shelves and perform many daily tasks such as cooking in homes that are not set up for people living with physical disabilities. The Tek robot can also be used outdoors, allowing users to travel over uneven streets, paths, slopes, and curbs and go for a walk with family or friends.

ROBOTS RISING UP!

Future wheelchair designs include a game-changing set of rubber tracks that move in and out, allowing the wheelchair to climb up and down stairs.

Devices like the Tek robot give people with walking difficulties more freedom and independence.

ALL ABOUT ARMS

Millions of people worldwide live without part of an arm. This can be the result of an accident, illness, or it may have been missing at birth. Today, some of these people have a robotic arm as a replacement, or prosthetic. Today's prosthetic arms perform as well as or sometimes even better than the real thing.

Learning to use a new robotic prosthetic arm takes time and patience.

MUSCLING IN ON THE ACTION

Our muscles make electrical signals when they move. When someone has lost the lower part of their arm, a myoelectric prosthetic lower arm can be controlled by electrical signals made by the muscles in the upper arm. Doctors place sensors that touch the muscles in the remaining part of the upper arm. The sensors are built into the prosthetic arm socket. The sensors capture the signals when muscles in the upper part of the arm twitch. A control unit translates the signals into commands for electric motors and joints to move the prosthetic lower arm and hand.

A prosthetic arm makes it possible to do everyday tasks again with ease.

ARMED AND READY

A prosthetic arm is usually made from a tough-but-light material called carbon fiber. The arm must have an open structure to let air flow, so the arm is not hot to wear. The arm has an adjustable opening to fit snugly onto the remaining part of the patient's limb. Motors inside are light and operate the wrist and fingers silently. Some people like their prosthetic arm to looks like that of a favorite robot, for example Iron Man. Others prefer rubbery skins to cover the working parts of the arm so the new arm blends in with the body.

ROBOTS RISING UP!

Myoelectric limbs can be very expensive to buy and so are not available to people in poorer parts of the world. But now it is possible to print them. A 3D printer can produce the parts for a plastic arm shell and jointed hand for about 100 dollars. It can do this at different scales for different sizes of wearer. The parts are joined with springs and wires. Once fitted with a motor and artificial tendons to operate the fingers, they are good to go.

EXOSUIT MIRACLE

People who thought they would never be able to walk again now can—by wearing a new robotic skeleton. An exoskeleton, or exosuit, can help people stand and move around independently on their own two feet once more.

ROBOTS RISING UP!

Walking up stairs, steps, or curbs is a different movement from walking. It involves lifting the body up or down. To do this, a ReWalk wearer switches to step mode by shifting their body or pressing buttons worn on the wrist. The exosuit then starts to carefully climb up or down the stairs as needed.

WALKER BOT

ReWalk is a robot that a person straps to their legs. It is a rigid belt with tough carbon fiber legs attached. The legs are **hinged** at the waist, knee, and ankle joints. The exosuit's joints are not powered by muscles and tendons, like human joints. Instead, each has an inbuilt battery-powered motor. The exosuit allows users to stand upright and then they can shift their body slightly to start it walking. The exosuit's joints then move the wearer's legs in a natural walking pattern.

Robotic exoskeletons are a game changer for many people with lower limb disabilities, including combat veterans.

Robotic suits can also help children who have walking difficulties to walk again.

CUSTOMIZED USE

We all walk differently. Some people take long **strides**, while other people walk with shorter strides. The exosuit's way of walking can be personalized by adjusting the system's inbuilt computer via the buttons on the wrist. This changes how much the joint motors move the exoskeleton, and with what force. The exosuit belt also contains a tilt sensor. The users can also instruct the computer to adjust how much they tilt their body to allow them to begin walking.

TRAINING TO WALK

Robots can also step in to help people learn how to walk again after a stroke. A stroke is a change in the flow of blood in the brain. It can affect different parts of the brain such as those controlling the way someone walks. Strokes often affect only one leg. ReStore is a lightweight robotic aid worn on the lower leg. It has powered cables at the front and back. These are attached to the foot and heel of the wearer's shoe. The cables can stiffen or relax in sequence. These movements bend the foot into different positions as part of a natural walking movement.

ROBOTIC EXOSKELETONS

In the future, using a robotic exoskeleton could be all in the mind for some people. When a person's spinal cord is damaged at the neck and they are paralyzed, they may not be able to use one or more of their limbs. But they can learn to control the limbs of a robotic exoskeleton using only their brainpower.

Sensors on the Brain

A paralyzed person's brain can still send commands to move limbs, but instead of the commands going to the limbs, they can be redirected to a robot. To do this, doctors first create 2-inch (5 cm) holes on either side of the skull on the part of the brain that controls motor function, or the ability to move muscles. Then doctors put sensors in the holes, with part of the sensors resting on the outer **membrane** of the brain. These sensors then sense brain commands.

Brain Games

Patients need some intensive brain training to control an exoskeleton. First, the patient plays a computer game using the messages from the sensors. In it they practice using their thoughts of movements to control the different limbs of a computer-simulated exoskeleton. Once this is working, the patient is connected to the actual exoskeleton.

Robotic exoskeletons can give people who never thought they would walk again the ability to do so on their own.

Regaining Movement

It is difficult to translate thoughts of human movements into robotic movements. For example, walking is not just about moving the legs up and down. It also involves balancing the body, so at first, people in the exoskeleton are suspended in a harness so they don't lose balance. In the future, exoskeletons will have inbuilt stabilizers so people don't topple over. It can take months to relearn natural movements such as walking and picking up objects but thanks to robots, it is at least possible.

Are Brain-Controlled Exoskeletons a Good or Bad Idea?

Many people believe using the mind to move an exoskeleton is a good idea. They say it allows people who thought they were paralyzed for life to move their bodies without help from others, so they can lead more independent lives. However, some people argue that this expensive technology will not help many paralyzed people globally. They think more money should be spent on research into how bodies can repair their own nervous system. Do you believe exoskeletons are a good investment or do you think the money should be spent elsewhere?

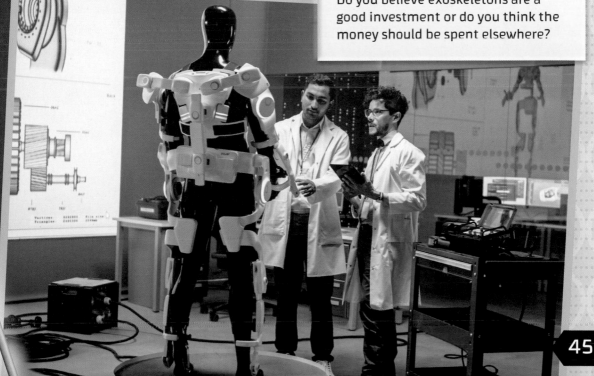

Engineers are working on new, improved robot exoskeletons all the time.

GLOSSARY

abnormalities things that are not normal

algae plantlike living things, such as seaweed

antibiotic a substance that treats infections and diseases caused by bacteria

circulatory system the system in the body that contains the heart and the blood vessels and moves blood throughout the body

database an organized collection of digital information, or data

depression an illness in which patients feel sad for a long period of time

diabetes a disease that occurs when a person's blood sugar is too high

diagnosis a judgment about what a particular illness or condition is

expressive showing what someone thinks or feels

high-definition very sharp and clear

hinged having two pieces joined together so that one of them can swing open and closed

humanoid like a human

joystick a device that can be moved forward, backward, and sideways to control a machine or computer

laser a very narrow beam of highly concentrated light

limitations things that cannot be done

magnified made to appear larger than it is

membrane a very thin skin or surface

multi-jointed having several joints, places where two or more parts are connected

navigation finding and following a route

nervous system the system in the body that sends messages back and forth between the brain and the rest of the body via nerves

pneumonia a serious type of lung infection

precision care and accuracy

prescription the details of what medicine needs to be taken and when to take it

prosthetic limbs artificial legs and arms that replace missing body parts

pulse the regular beating of the heart

pulses short bursts

radio waves invisible forms of energy that can carry information through the air

remote far away from where people live

sample a small amount of something that gives you information about the thing it was taken from

sensors devices that sense things such as heat or movement

side effects extra and often bad effects that a medicine has on a patient

silicon a substance found in sand that is used to make computer and electronic parts

simulate to do or make something that looks real but is not real

strides walking steps

symptoms signs of an illness

tumors abnormal swellings of parts of the body

ultraviolet (UV) a type of energy produced by the Sun and some artificial sources

virtual reality (VR) a computer-generated world that feels real and can be explored and interacted with by a person

FIND OUT MORE

BOOKS

Drimmer, Stephanie Warren. *Ultimate Book of the Future: Incredible, Ingenious, and Totally Real Tech That Will Change Life as You Know It*. National Geographic Kids, 2022.

Leavitt, Amie Jane. *Dream Jobs If You Like Robots* (Dream Jobs for Future You). Capstone Press, 2020.

Whiting, Jim. *Robots* (Odysseys in Technology). Creative Education, 2020.

WEBSITES

Discover more about robots at:
https://kids.britannica.com/kids/article/robot/353723

Learn more about how robots work at:
https://science.howstuffworks.com/robot.htm

Find out more about robots at:
https://sciencetrek.org/sciencetrek/topics/robots/facts.cfm

Read more about medical robots at:
www.brainlab.com/journal/types-of-medical-robots-in-use-today-and-in-the-future

Publisher's note to educators and parents:
All the websites featured above have been carefully reviewed to ensure that they are suitable for students. However, many websites change often, and we cannot guarantee that a site's future contents will continue to meet our high standards of educational value. Please be advised that students should be closely monitored whenever they access the Internet.

INDEX

3D printing 41

artificial intelligence (AI)
    8–9, 27, 31
augmented reality (AR) 15
autonomous 19, 26, 29, 32, 34

cameras 6, 12, 18, 20–21, 31, 37
care homes 25, 29, 30–31
circulatory system 22
communication 5, 6, 10, 11, 29,
    30, 31, 33, 35
controllers/operators 12, 14,
    15, 16, 17, 18, 21, 22–23, 33, 37,
    39, 40, 42, 43, 44–45

diagnosis 4, 5, 6, 7, 8, 9, 10–11,
    21, 31
drones 36–37
drugs 4, 9, 10, 20–21, 22, 23,
    24–25, 26, 27, 32, 34, 36–37

examinations 6, 7, 20
exosuits 42–43, 44–45

face recognition 29

haptic feedback
    technology 14
hospitals 4, 6, 7, 12–17, 24, 25,
    26, 27, 28, 31, 32–33, 34–35,
    36
humanoids 5, 8, 10–11, 28, 29,
    30–31, 35

infection 5, 8, 9, 13, 22, 23, 33
injections 4, 23, 28

LiDAR 26, 35

magnetism 8, 21, 22, 23
microphones 6
mistakes 5, 8, 19, 24–25

navigation 6, 26, 27, 32,
    34–35, 37
nervous system 23, 45

pharmacies 24–25
programming 9, 19, 30, 33, 34
prosthetic limbs 4, 40–41

rehabilitation 38–45
remote areas 7
robotic arms 12–13, 16–17, 18,
    24, 27, 38, 40–41
robotic cleaners 32–33
robotic exoskeletons 42–45
robotic nurses 26–31
robotic pharmacists 24–25
robotic pills 20–21
robotic porters 34–35
robotic surgeons 12–19

safety 5, 9, 14, 15, 19, 25, 38
scans 8, 9, 20
sensors 6, 18, 26, 31, 32, 35, 37,
    40, 43, 44
sonar 26, 35
surgery 4, 9, 12–19, 28, 31, 35,
    38
    minimally invasive 13, 18–19
    open 13
    training 14–15, 18

telemedics 6–7
treatment 4, 5, 7, 8, 20–25,
    28, 31, 33, 34, 36–37, 38

virtual reality (VR) 14–15, 18
voice recognition 29

X-rays 8, 9, 15, 35

ABOUT THE AUTHOR

Louise Spilsbury is an award-winning children's book author who has written hundreds of books about science and technology. In writing and researching this book, she has discovered that robots are rising, revolutionizing our world, and paving the way for an awesome high-tech future!